Celebrating
OHIO

The text of this book is set in Weidemann.
The display type is set in Bernard Gothic.
The illustrations are drawn with pencil and colored digitally.
The maps are pen, ink, and watercolor.

Library of Congress Cataloging-in-Publication Data
Kurtz, Jane.
Celebrating Ohio / Jane Kurtz, C. B. Canga.
p. cm. — (Green light readers level 3)
Includes bibliographical references and index.
Audience: Grades K–3.
ISBN 978-0-544-41979-7 paperback
ISBN 978-0-544-42282-7 paper over board
1. Ohio—Juvenile literature. I. Canga, C. B., illustrator. II. Title.
F491.3.K87 2015
977.1—dc23
2014045

Manufactured in China
SCP 10 9 8 7 6 5 4 3 2 1
4500536551

50 STATES TO CELEBRATE

Celebrating
OHIO

Written by **Jane Kurtz**
Illustrated by **C. B. Canga**

Green Light Readers

Houghton Mifflin Harcourt

Boston   New York

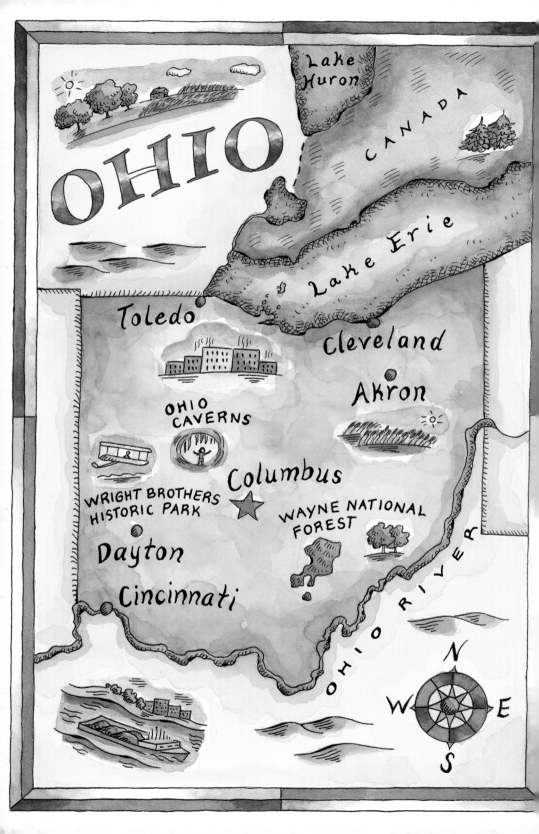

Hi, I'm Mr. Geo!

I'm exploring a state in the Midwest.

It shares its name with a mighty river.

The **Iroquois** called the river "Ohi-yo."

That's right! I'm in Ohio.

The Ohio River separates Ohio from
Kentucky and West Virginia.

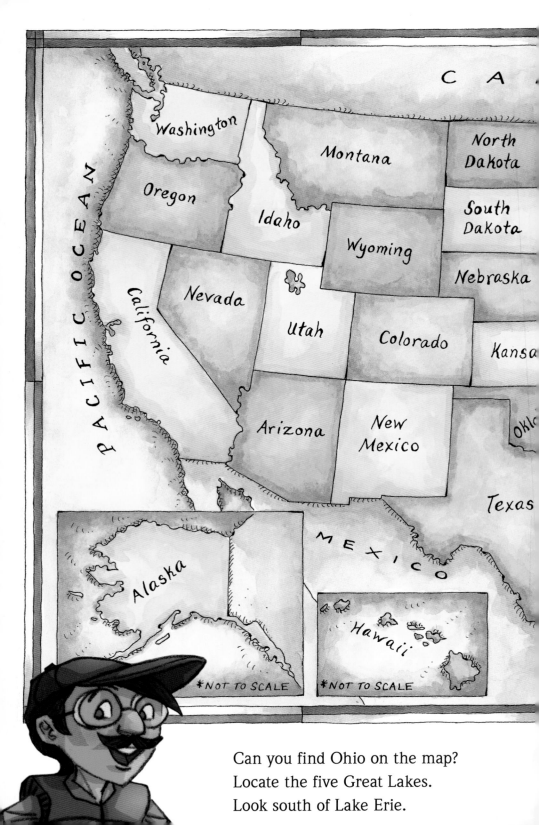

Can you find Ohio on the map?
Locate the five Great Lakes.
Look south of Lake Erie.

Now look west of Pennsylvania,
north of Kentucky and West Virginia, and east of Indiana.
Ohio is right there.

Welcome to Columbus, the state capital.
It's time for the Ohio State Fair.
The best place to begin is sky high.
I can see everything from here.

Parades!

Rides!

Games!

Prizes!

Even the horse and pony shows!

The fair celebrates Ohio's **agricultural** roots.
I think I can climb to the top
of this gigantic corn wall . . .

. . . but I'm not sure if I can win this mini tractor pull!

There are life-size cow **sculptures** made of butter at the Ohio State Fair.

Farming is big business in Ohio.
Fields full of corn, wheat, and soybeans.
Chicken coops full of eggs.
Barns full of cows!

Did you know?

Ohio farmers are among the country's leading growers of tomatoes and pumpkins.

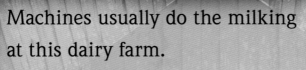

Machines usually do the milking
at this dairy farm.
But my farmer friend is showing us
how to milk the old-fashioned way.
Whoops! Another squirt in the eye!

Ohio is a top producer of Swiss cheese
in the United States.

I love seeing how things are made.
Ohio's many factories produce lots of items.
This **factory** makes shiny metal whistles.
Tweeeeeeet!

Other products made in Ohio are tires, jeeps, footballs, playhouses, paint, washing machines, flashlights, and batteries.

Ah! This factory
has a very sweet smell.
It makes millions of lollipops every day.
My favorite flavor?
Blue raspberry!

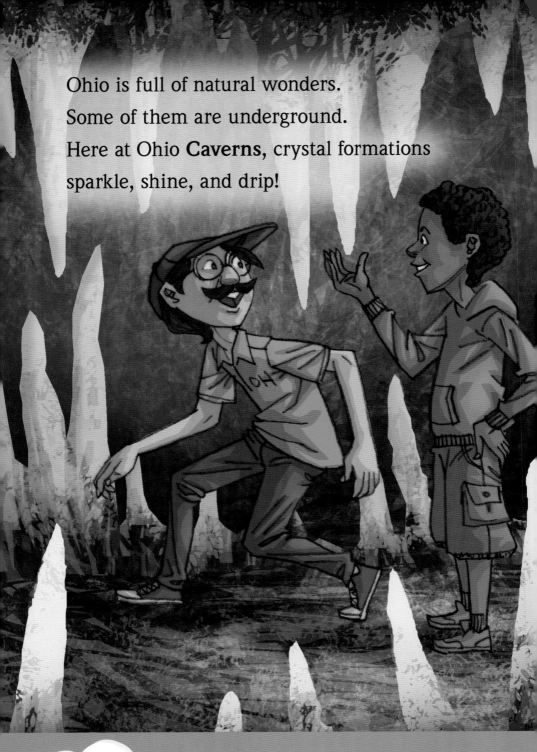

Ohio is full of natural wonders.
Some of them are underground.
Here at Ohio **Caverns,** crystal formations
sparkle, shine, and drip!

Did you know?

Salt and coal are mined from some
of Ohio's caves.

Now I'm enjoying the trees and trails
of Wayne National Forest.
Stop!
Wild turkeys crossing!

Did you know?

Ohio is called the Buckeye State because
buckeye trees grow here. The nut of a buckeye
tree looks like the eye of a male deer (a buck).   13

Lakes and rivers are important
natural resources in Ohio.
To the north, Lake Erie's long coast
is home to big cities and busy ports.
What I like best?
Paddling around the islands.

The wide Ohio River marks
the state's southern border.
Join me for some old-style cruising!
First, a canal boat pulled by mules.
Next, a riverboat powered by paddle wheel.

Did you know? The city of Cincinnati is located on the Ohio River.

Native Americans known as Mound Builders
were among the first people in Ohio.
Some built a huge serpent-shaped
mound out of the earth.
From up here, I can see its curly coils.

The Great Serpent Mound is about
1,348 feet long.

French explorers and fur traders
were the first Europeans to see Ohio.
The British came next.
Later, American **pioneers** moved to Ohio.
They traveled from the East in covered wagons.

Johnny "Appleseed" Chapman was one of
Ohio's most famous pioneers. He planted lots
of apple trees in the state.

At Historic Sauder Village, costumed guides show us how settlers lived and worked in the 1800s. I'm learning how to spin wool into thread. It's trickier than I thought!

Around the time of the **Civil War,**
thousands of enslaved Africans
hid here at the Rankin House.
It was a safe stop on the **Underground Railroad.**

The Underground Railroad was not a real railroad.
It was a system of routes and hiding places that
brought enslaved people north to freedom.

At the National Underground Railroad
Freedom Center, I heard stories about
heroes and courage.
I admire the people who escaped slavery
and those who helped them.

Ohio has many more museums full of history.
In Dayton, I learned about the **Wright brothers.**
They invented the first successful airplane.
But they started out building bikes.
Is this bike a little wobbly . . . or is it me?

THE WRIGHT

Space travel thrills me too.
At Cincinnati's science museum
I took control of a **Mars rover**.
At Cleveland's Great Lakes Science Center,
I sat in a space capsule.
Does this suit look good on me?

Did you know?

John Glenn, the first person to orbit the earth, and Neil Armstrong, the first person to walk on the moon, were both born in Ohio.

23

I have visited the homes of many
United States presidents.
But this historic site is about our **first ladies.**
I enjoyed stories about first ladies and their pets.
Grace Coolidge had a pet raccoon!
Dolley Madison liked to greet guests
with a parrot perched on her shoulder!

Seven first ladies were from Ohio.
Eight American presidents were too.

Now I'm ready to rock and roll!
The Rock and Roll Hall of Fame in Cleveland
is the perfect place to feel the beat!

Visiting Ohio Village feels like
taking a trip back in time.
The Ohio Village Muffins play baseball
the way it was played in 1860.

Funny hats!
Floppy bow ties!
Jumbo-size baseballs!
No mitts!
I hope I can catch with my bare hands!

 Ohio's two major-league baseball teams are the Cleveland Indians and the Cincinnati Reds.

Are you ready for some football?
At the Professional Football Hall of Fame,
I can review the highlights
of every Super Bowl game!

Did you know?

The Professional Football Hall of Fame is in Canton, Ohio, because that's where the National Football League (NFL) was formed in 1920.

Now it's time to put on my game face!
I cheer the Browns when I am in Cleveland.
I root for the Bengals when I am in Cincinnati.
And wherever I go in this great state, I shout
"Hip Hip Hooray" for the Ohio State Buckeyes!

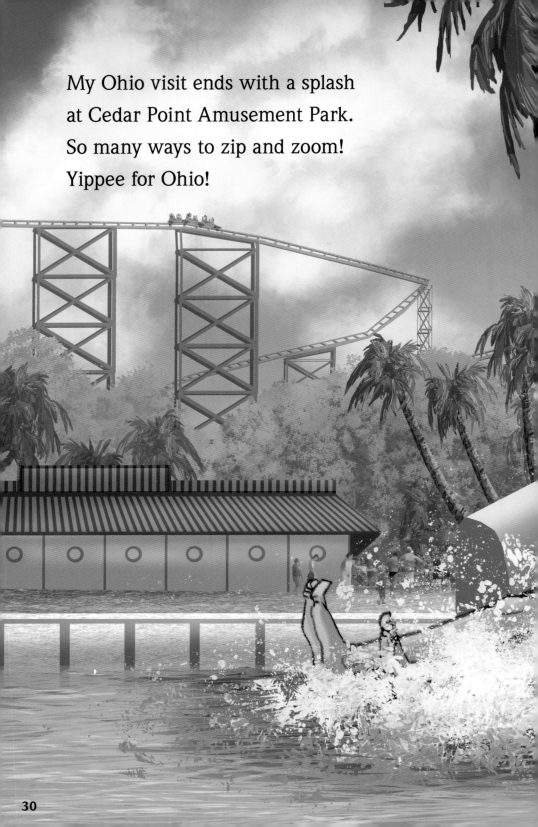

My Ohio visit ends with a splash
at Cedar Point Amusement Park.
So many ways to zip and zoom!
Yippee for Ohio!

Fast Facts About Ohio

Nickname: The Buckeye State

State motto: With God All Things Are Possible

State capital: Columbus

Other major cities: Cleveland, Cincinnati, Toledo, Akron, Dayton

Year of statehood: 1803

State mammal: White-tailed deer

State bird: Cardinal

State flower: Scarlet carnation

State flag:

Population: 11.3 million, according to the 2013 U.S. Census.

Fun facts: Ohio was home to eight presidents before they were elected to office. They include William Henry Harrison, Ulysses S. Grant, Rutherford B. Hayes, James Garfield, Benjamin Harrison, William McKinley, William H. Taft, and Warren G. Harding.

Dates in Ohio History

1000–1500: Early Native American groups lived in an area now called Ohio.

1669: The French explorer La Salle travels the Ohio region.

1754–63: The French and British battle during the French and Indian War; Great Britain wins and takes control of the Ohio area.

1787: Ohio becomes part of the United States' Northwest Territory.

1788: Marietta becomes first permanent U.S. settlement in an area of the Northwest Territory that later becomes the state of Ohio.

1803: Ohio becomes a state.

1832: Work is completed on the Ohio and Erie canals.

1850: Ohio holds its first state fair.

1861–65: Ohio becomes an important stop on the Underground Railroad.

1870–1900: Ohio's location, transportation systems, and natural resources create a period of industrial and urban growth.

1903: The Wright brothers, from Dayton, Ohio, are the first to successfully fly a powered plane.

1962: Ohio's John Glenn is the first American to orbit Earth.

1963: The Professional Football Hall of Fame opens in Canton.

1969: Ohio's Neil Armstrong is the first person to walk on the moon.

1995: The Rock and Roll Hall of Fame opens in Cleveland.

2004: The National Underground Railroad Freedom Center opens.

Activities

1. **LOCATE** the five states that border Ohio. Which state is to the north? Which one is to the east? Which ones are to the south? Which one is to the west? **SAY** the name of each state out loud.

2. **DESIGN** a postcard to send to a friend about Ohio. On the front include a picture of something to see or do in Ohio. On the back, include a message that gives an interesting fact about Ohio.

3. **SHARE** two facts you learned about Ohio with a family member or friend.

4. **PRETEND** you are at the Ohio State Fair. A booth with really awesome prizes is holding a trivia contest about Ohio. If you get all the answers right, you can pick any prize you want from the booth.

   a. **WHERE** is the Ohio State Fair held?

   b. **WHAT** are three agricultural products grown on farms in Ohio?

   c. **WHICH** of the Great Lakes borders northern Ohio?

   d. **WHO** was the pioneer who planted lots of apple trees in Ohio?

5. **UNJUMBLE** these words that have something to do with Georgia. Write your answers on a separate sheet of paper.

   a. **YBSONAES** (HINT: an Ohio crop)

   b. **STYRALC** (HINT: found in Ohio caves)

   c. **LVADLECEN** (HINT: a big city on a Lake)

   d. **EIPRSOEN** (HINT: settlers)

   e. **CATROFEIS** (HINT: where some products are made)

   FOR ANSWERS, SEE PAGE 36.

Glossary

agricultural: having to do with farms or farming. (p. 6)

cavern: a very large cave. (p. 12)

Civil War: the war between the Northern states and the Southern states that helped end slavery in the United States. (p. 20)

factory: a building in which products are manufactured or assembled. (p. 10)

first lady: the wife of a U.S. president. (p. 24)

Iroquois: Native American people originally from the northeastern part of what is now the United States, including much of New York; some Iroquois eventually moved as far west as the Ohio River Valley. (p. 1)

Mars rover: a robotic vehicle that travels on the surface of Mars, gathering scientific information; at Columbus, Ohio's Center of Science and Industry (COSI), visitors can guide a radio-controlled wheeled rover on a simulated Martian surface. (p. 23)

natural resources: something found in nature that is necessary or useful to people; water, forests, coal, and oil are all natural resources. (p. 14)

pioneer: a person who is first to settle in a region. (p. 18)

sculpture: a figure or other design that is made by sculpting clay or carving wood, marble, ice, or another material; at the Ohio State Fair, people create sculptures from butter. (p. 7)

Underground Railroad: a system of escape routes and hiding places used to bring enslaved people north to freedom. (p. 20)

Wright brothers: Wilbur and Orville Wright were inventors who designed and successfully flew the first powered airplane in 1903. (p. 22)

Answers to Activities on page 34:

1) Michigan is to the north, Pennsylvania is to the east, West Virginia is also to the east, but mainly to the south, Kentucky and West Virginia are to the south, Indiana is to the west; 2) postcards will vary; 3) answers will vary; 4a) Columbus (the state capital), 4b) corn, soy, and wheat (tomatoes and pumpkins are also acceptable answers), 4c) Lake Erie, 4d) John Chapman, also known as Johnny Appleseed; 5a) SOYBEANS, 5b) CRYSTAL, 5c) CLEVELAND, 5d) PIONEERS, 5e) FACTORIES.